T0145563

Morning
and Evening
Thoughts

JAMES ALLEN TITLES

Above Life's Turmoil

All These Things Added

As a Man Thinketh

Byways of Blessedness

Eight Pillars of Prosperity

Foundation Stones to Happiness and Success

From Passion to Peace

From Poverty to Power

James Allen's Book of Meditations for Every Day in the Year

Light on Life's Difficulties

Man: King of Mind, Body, and Circumstance

Men and Systems

Morning and Evening Thoughts

Out from the Heart

Poems of Peace

The Life Triumphant

The Mastery of Destiny

The Shining Gateway

Through the Gate of Good

Morning
and Evening
Thoughts

James Allen

Published 2019 by Gildan Media LLC
aka G&D Media
www.GandDmedia.com

Design by Meghan Day Healey of Story Horse, LLC

Library of Congress Cataloging-in-Publication Data is available upon request

ISBN: 978-1-7225-0240-9

10   9   8   7   6   5   4   3   2   1

Conquer thyself,
Then thou shalt know;
Climb to the high,
Leave thou the low.
Deliverance
Shall him entrance
Who strives with sins and sorrows,
tears and pains.
Till he attains.

–James Allen

First Morning

In aiming at the life of blessedness, one of the simplest beginnings to be considered, and rightly made, is that which we all make every day—namely, the beginning of each day's life. There is a sense in which every day may be regarded as the beginning of a new life, in which one can think, act, and live newly, and in a wiser and better spirit. The right beginning of the day will be followed by cheerfulness permeating the household with a sunny influence, and the tasks and duties of the day will be undertaken in a strong and confident spirit, and the whole day will be well lived.

First Evening

There can be no progress, no achievement, without sacrifice, and a man's worldly success will be in the measure that he sacrifices his confused animal thoughts, and fixes his mind on the development of his plans, and on the strengthening of his resolution and self-reliance. And the higher he lifts his thoughts, the more manly, upright, and righteous he becomes, the greater will be his success, the more blessed and enduring will be his achievements.

None but right acts can follow right thoughts; none but a right life can follow right acts; and by living a right life all blessedness is achieved.

> Mind is the Master-power that moulds and makes.
> And Man is Mind, and evermore he takes
> The Tool of Thought, and, shaping what he wills,
> Brings forth a thousand joys, a thousand ills;—
> He thinks in secret, and it comes to pass;
> Environment is but his looking-glass.

Second Evening

Calmness of mind is one of the beautiful jewels of wisdom. A man becomes calm in the measure that he understands himself as a thought-evolved being . . . and as he develops a right understanding, and sees more and more clearly the internal relations of things by the action of cause and effect, he ceases to fret and fume, and worry and grieve, and remains poised, steadfast, serene.

Third Morning

To follow, under all circumstances, the highest promptings within you; to be always true to the divine self; to rely upon the inward Voice, the inward Light, and to pursue your purpose with a fearless and restful heart, believing that the future will yield unto you the need of every thought and effort; knowing that the laws of the universe can never fail, and that your own will come back to you with mathematical exactitude—this is faith and the living of faith.

Third Evening

Have a thorough understanding of your work, and let it be your own; and as you proceed, ever following the inward Guide, the infallible Voice, you will pass on from victory to victory, and will rise step by step to higher resting-places, and your ever-broadening outlook will gradually reveal to you the essential beauty and purpose of life. Self-purified, health will be yours; self-governed, power will be yours, and all that you do will prosper.

> And I may stand where health, success, and power
> Await my coming, if, each fleeting hour,
> I cling to love and patience; and abide
> With stainlessness; and never step aside
> From high integrity; so shall I see
> At last the land of immortality.

Fourth Morning

When the tongue is well controlled and wisely subdued; when selfish impulses and unworthy thoughts no longer rush to the tongue demanding utterance; when the speech has become harmless, pure, gracious, gentle, and purposeful, and no word is uttered but in sincerity and truth—then are the five steps in virtuous speech accomplished, then is the second great lesson in Truth learned and mastered.

Make pure thy heart, and thou wilt make thy life
Rich, sweet and beautiful.

Fourth Evening

Having clothed himself with humility, the first questions a man asks himself are:—"How am I acting toward others?" "What am I doing to others?" "How am I thinking of others?" "Are my thoughts of, and acts toward, others prompted by unselfish love?" As a man, in the silence of his soul, asks himself these searching questions, he will unerringly see where he has hitherto failed.

Fifth Morning

To dwell in love always and toward all is to live the true life, is to have Life itself. Knowing this, the good man gives up himself unreservedly to the Spirit of Love, and dwells in Love toward all, contending with none, condemning none, but loving all.

The Christ Spirit of Love puts an end, not only to all sin, but to all division and contention.

Fifth Evening

When sin and self are abandoned, the heart is restored to its imperishable Joy.

Joy comes and fills the self-emptied heart; it abides with the peaceful; its reign is with the pure.

Joy flees from the selfish, it deserts the quarrelsome; it is hidden from the impure.

Joy cannot remain with the selfish; it is wedded to Love.

Sixth Morning

In the pure heart there is no room left where personal judgments and hatreds can find lodgment, for it is filled to overflowing with tenderness and love; it sees no evil, and only as men succeed in seeing no evil in others will they become free from sin, and sorrow, and suffering.

If men only understood
That the heart that sins must sorrow,
That the hateful mind tomorrow
Reaps its barren harvest, weeping,
Starving, resting not, nor sleeping;
Tenderness would fill their being,
They would see with Pity's seeing
If they only understood.

Sixth Evening

To stand face to face with truth; to arrive, after innumerable wanderings and pains, at wisdom and bliss; not to be finally defeated and cast out, but to ultimately triumph over every inward foe—such is man's divine destiny, such his glorious goal; and this, every saint, sage, and savior has declared.

A man only begins to be a man when he ceases to whine and revile, and commences to search for the hidden justice which regulates his life. And as he adapts his mind to that regulating factor, he ceases to accuse others as the cause of his condition, and builds himself up in strong and noble thoughts; ceases to kick against circumstances; but begins to use them as aids to his more rapid progress, and as a means of discovering the hidden powers and possibilities within himself.

Seventh Morning

The will to evil and the will to good
Are both within thee, which wilt thou employ?
Thou knowest what is right and what is wrong,
Which wilt thou love and foster? which destroy?
Thou art the chooser of thy thoughts and deeds;
Thou art the maker of thine inward state;
The power is thine to be what thou wilt be;
Thou buildest Truth and Love, or lies and hate.

Seventh Evening

The teaching of Jesus brings men back to the simple truth that righteousness, or *right-doing*, is entirely a matter of individual conduct, and not a mystical something apart from a man's thoughts and deeds.

Calmness and patience can become habitual by first grasping, through effort, a calm and patient thought, and then continuously thinking it, and living in it, until "use becomes second nature," and anger and impatience pass away for ever.

Eighth Morning

Man is made or unmade by himself; in the armoury of thought he forges the weapons by which he destroys himself; he also fashions the tools with which he builds for himself heavenly mansions of joy and strength and peace. By the right choice and true application of thought man ascends to the Divine Perfection; by the abuse and wrong application of thought he descends below the level of the beast. Between these two extremes are all the grades of character, and man is their maker and master.

As a being of Power, Intelligence, and Love, and the lord of his own thoughts, man holds the key to every situation.

Eighth Evening

Whatsoever you harbour in the inmost chambers of your heart will, sooner or later, by the inevitable law of reaction, shape itself in your outward life.

Every soul attracts its own, and nothing can possibly come to it that does not belong to it. To realize this is to recognize the universality of Divine Law.

> If thou would'st right the world,
> And banish all its evils and its woes.
> Make its wild places bloom,
> And its drear deserts blossom as the rose—
> Then right thyself.

Ninth Morning

Whatever conditions are rendering your life burdensome, you may pass out of and beyond them by developing and utilizing within you the transforming power of self-purification and self-conquest.

Before the divine radiance of a pure heart all darkness vanishes and all clouds melt away, and he who has conquered self has conquered the universe.

He who sets his foot firmly upon the path of self-conquest, who walks, aided by the staff of faith, the highway of self-sacrifice, will assuredly achieve the highest prosperity, and will reap abounding and enduring joy and bliss.

Ninth Evening

It is the silent and conquering thought-forces which bring all things into manifestation. The universe grew out of thought.

To adjust all your thoughts to a perfect and unswerving faith in the omnipotence and supremacy of Good, is to co-operate with that Good, and to realize within yourself the solution and destruction of all evil.

To mentally deny evil is not sufficient; it must, by daily practice, be risen above and understood. To affirm the Good mentally is inadequate; it must, by unswerving endeavor, be entered into and comprehended.

Tenth Morning

Every thought you think is a force sent out.

Whatever your position in life may be, before you can hope to enter into any measure of success, usefulness, and power, you must learn how to focus your thought-forces by cultivating calmness and repose.

There is no difficulty, however great, but will yield before a calm and purposeful concentration of thought, and no legitimate object but may be speedily actualized by the intelligent use and direction of one's soul-forces.

Think good thoughts, and they will quickly become actualized in your outward life in the form of good conditions.

Tenth Evening

That which you would be and hope to be, you may be now. Non-accomplishment resides in your perpetual postponement, and, having the power to postpone, you also have the power to accomplish—to perpetually accomplish: Realize this truth, and you shall be today, and every day, the ideal being of whom you dreamed.

Say to yourself, "I will live in my Ideal now; I will manifest my Ideal now; I will be my Ideal now; and all that tempts me away from my Ideal I will not listen to; I will listen only to the voice of my Ideal."

Eleventh Morning

Be as a flower, content to be, to grow in sweetness day by day.

If thou would'st perfect thyself in knowledge, perfect thyself in Love. If thou would'st reach the Highest, ceaselessly cultivate a loving and compassionate heart.

To him who choose Goodness, sacrificing all, is given that which is more than, and includes, all.

Eleventh Evening

The Great Law never cheats any man of his just due.

Human life, when rightly lived, is simple with a beautiful simplicity.

He who comprehends the utter simplicity of life, who obeys its laws, and does not step aside into the dark paths and complex mazes of selfish desire, stands where no harm can reach him.

Then there is fulness of joy, abounding plenty, and rich and complete blessedness.

Twelfth Morning

Every man reaps the results of his own thoughts and deeds, and suffers for his own wrong.

He who begins right, and continues right, does not need to desire and search for felicitous results; they are already at hand; they follow as consequences; they are the certainties, the realities, of life.

Sweet is the rest and deep the bliss of him who has freed his heart from its lusts and hatreds and dark desires.

Twelfth Evening

You are the creator of your own shadows; you desire, and then you grieve; renounce, and then you shall rejoice.

Of all the beautiful truths pertaining to the soul, . . . none is more gladdening or fruitful of divine promise and confidence than this—that man is the master of thought, the moulder of character, and the maker and shaper of character, environment, and destiny.

Thirteenth Morning

As darkness is a passing shadow, and light is substance that remains, so sorrow is fleeting, but joy abides for ever. No true thing can pass away and become lost; no false thing can remain and be preserved. Sorrow is false, and it can not live; Joy is true, and it can not die. Joy may become hidden for a time, but it can always be recovered; sorrow may remain for a period, but it can be transcended and dispersed.

Do not think your sorrow will remain; it will pass away like a cloud. Do not believe that the torments of sin are ever your portion; they will vanish like a hideous nightmare. Awake! Arise! Be holy and joyful.

Thirteenth Evening

Tribulation lasts only so long as there remains some chaff of self which needs to be removed. The *tribulum*, or threshing machine, ceases to work when all the grain is separated from the chaff; and when the last impurities are blown away from the soul, tribulation has completed its work, and there is no more need for it; then abiding joy is realized.

The sole and supreme use of suffering is to purify, to burn out all that is useless and impure. Suffering ceases for him who is pure. There can be no object in burning gold after the dross had been removed.

Fourteenth Morning

In speaking of self-control, one is easily misunderstood. It should not be associated with a destructive repression, but with a constructive expression.

A man is happy, wise and great in the measure that he controls himself; he is wretched, foolish, and mean in the measure that he allows his animal nature to dominate his thoughts and actions.

He who controls himself, controls his life, his circumstances, his destiny; and wherever he goes he carries his happiness with him as an abiding possession.

Renunciation precedes regeneration.

The permanent happiness which men seek in dissipation, excitement, and abandonment to unworthy pleasures, is found only in the life which reverses all this—the life of self-control.

Fourteenth Evening

Law, not confusion, is the dominating principle in the universe; justice, not injustice, is the soul and substance of life; and righteousness, not corruption, is the moulding and moving force in the spiritual government of the world. This being so, man has but to right himself to find that the universe is right.

> When I am pure,
> I shall have solved the mystery of life;
> I shall be sure,
> When I am free from hatred, lust and strife,
> I am in Truth, and Truth abides in me;
> I shall be safe, and sane, and wholly free,
> When I am pure.

Fifteenth Morning

If men only understood.
That their hatred and resentment.
Slays their peace and sweet contentment
Hurts themselves, helps not another,
Does not cheer one lonely brother,
They would seek the better doing
Of good deeds which leaves no rueing—
    If they only understood.

If men only understood
How Love conquers; how prevailing
Is its might, grim hate assailing;
How compassion endeth sorrow,
Maketh wise, and doth not borrow
Pain of passion, they would ever
Live in Love, in hatred never:—
    If they only understood.

Fifteenth Evening

The grace and beauty that were in Jesus can be of no value to you—cannot be understood by you—unless they are also *in you*, and they can never be in you, until you practice them, for, apart from *doing*, the qualities which constitute Goodness do not, as far as you are concerned, exist. To adore Jesus for his good qualities is a long step toward Truth, but to practice those qualities is Truth itself; and he who truly adores the perfection of another will not rest content in his own imperfection, but will fashion his soul after the likeness of that other.

Therefore thou who adorest Jesus for his divine qualities, practice those qualities thyself, and thou too shalt be divine.

Sixteenth Morning

Let a man realize that life in its totality proceeds from the mind, and lo, the way of blessedness is opened up to him! For he will then discover that he possesses the power to rule his mind, and to fashion it in accordance with his Ideal. So will he elect to strongly and steadfastly walk those pathways of thought and action which are altogether excellent; to him life will become beautiful and sacred; and, sooner or later, he will put to flight all evil, confusion, and suffering; for it is impossible for a man to fall short of liberation, enlightenment, and peace, who guards with unwearying diligence the gateway of his heart.

Sixteenth Evening

By constantly overcoming self, a man gains a knowledge of the subtle intricacies of his mind; and it is this divine knowledge which enables him to become established in calmness. Without self-knowledge there can be no abiding peace of mind, and those who are carried away by tempestuous passions, cannot approach the holy place where calmness reigns. The weak man is like one who, having mounted a fiery steed, allows it to run away with him, and carry him whithersoever it wills; the strong main is like one who, having mounted the steed, governs it with a masterly hand, and makes it go in whatever direction and at whatever speed he commands.

Seventeenth Morning

There is no strife, no selfishness, in the Kingdom; there is perfect harmony, equipoise, and rest.

Those who live in the Kingdom of Love, have all their needs supplied by the Law of Love.

As self is the root cause of all strife and suffering, so Love is the root cause of all peace and bliss.

Those who are at rest in the Kingdom, do not look for happiness in any outward possessions. They are freed from all anxiety and trouble, and resting in Love, they are the embodiment of happiness.

Seventeenth Evening

L et it not be supposed that the children of the Kingdom live in ease and indolence (these two sins are the first that have to be eradicated when the search for the Kingdom is entered upon); they live in a peaceful activity; in fact, they only truly live, for the life of self, with its train of worries, griefs, and fears, is not *real life*.

The children of the Kingdom are *known by their life*, they manifest the fruits of the Spirit—"Love, joy, peace, long-suffering, kindness, goodness, faithfulness, meekness, temperance, self-control"—under all circumstances and all vicissitudes.

Eighteenth Morning

The gospel of Jesus is a gospel of *living and doing*. If it were not this it would not voice the Eternal Truth. Its Temple is *Purified Conduct*, the entrance-door to which is *Self-Surrender*. It invites men to shake off sin, and promises, as a result, joy and blessedness and perfect peace.

The Kingdom of Heaven is perfect trust, perfect knowledge, perfect peace. . . . No sin can enter therein, no self-born thought or deed can pass its golden gates; no impure desire can defile its radiant robes. . . . All may enter it who will, but all must pay the price—*the unconditional abandonment of self.*

Eighteenth Evening

I say this—and know it to be truth—*that circumstances can only affect you in so far as you allow them to do so.* You are swayed by circumstances because you have not a right understanding of the nature, use, and power of thought. You believe (and upon this little word *belief* hang all our joys and sorrows) that outward things have the power to make or mar your life; by so doing you submit to those outward things, confess that you are their slave, and they your unconditional master. By so doing you invest them with a power which they do not of themselves possess, and you succumb, in reality not to the circumstances, but to the gloom or gladness, the fear or hope, the strength or weakness, which your thought-sphere has thrown around them.

Nineteenth Morning

If you are one of those who are praying for, and looking forward to, a happier world beyond the grave, here is a message of gladness for you—you may enter into and realize that happy world now; it fills the whole universe, and it is within you, waiting for you to find, acknowledge, and possess. Said one who understood the inner laws of Being— "When men shall say, lo here, or lo there, go not after them. The Kingdom of God is within you."

Nineteenth Evening

Heaven and hell are inward states. Sink into self and all its gratifications, and you sink into hell; rise above self into that state of consciousness which is the utter denial and forgetfulness of self and you enter Heaven.

So long as you persist in selfishly seeking for your own personal happiness, so long will happiness elude you, and you will be sowing the seeds of wretchedness. In so far as you succeed in losing yourself in the service of others, in that measure will happiness come to you, and you will reap a harvest of bliss.

Twentieth Morning

Sympathy given can never be wasted.

One aspect of sympathy is that of pity—pity for the distressed or pain-stricken, with a desire to alleviate or help them in their sufferings. The world needs more of this divine quality.

> For pity makes the world
> Soft to the weak, and noble for the strong.

Another form of sympathy is that of rejoicing with others who are more successful than ourselves, as though their success were our own.

Twentieth Evening

Sweet are companionships, pleasures, and material comforts, but they change and fade away. Sweeter still are Purity, Wisdom, and the knowledge of Truth, and these never change nor fade away.

He who has attained to the possession of spiritual things can never be deprived of his source of happiness; he will never have to part company with it, and wherever he goes in the whole universe, he will carry his possessions with him. His spiritual end will be the fulness of joy.

Twenty-First Morning

Let your heart grow and expand with ever-broadening love, until, freed from all hatred, and passion, and condemnation, it embraces the whole universe with thoughtful tenderness. As the flower opens its petals to receive the morning light, so open your soul more and more to the glorious light of Truth. Soar upward on the wings of aspiration; be fearless, and believe in the loftiest possibilities.

Twenty-First Evening

Mind clothes itself in garments of its own making. Mind is the arbiter of life; it is the creator and shaper of conditions, and the recipient of its own results. It contains within itself both the power to create illusion and to perceive reality.

Mind is the infallible weaver of destiny; thought is the thread, good and evil deeds are the warp and woof; and the web, woven upon the loom of life, is character.

Make pure thy heart, and thou wilt make thy life
Rich, sweet, and beautiful, unmarred by strife.

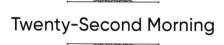

Twenty-Second Morning

Cherish your visions; cherish your ideals; cherish the music that stirs in your heart, the beauty that forms in your mind, the loveliness that drapes your purest thoughts, for out of them will grow all delightful conditions, all heavenly environment; of these, if you will remain true to them, your world will at last be built.

Guard well thy mind, and, noble, strong, and free,
Nothing shall harm, disturb or conquer thee;
For all thy foes are in thy heart and mind,
There also thy salvation thou shalt find.

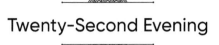

Twenty-Second Evening

Dream lofty dreams, and as you dream so shall you become. Your vision is the promise of what you shall one day be; your Ideal is the prophecy of what you shall at last unveil.

The greatest achievement was at first and for a time a dream. The oak sleeps in the acorn; the bird waits in the egg; and in the highest vision of the soul a waking angel stirs.

Your circumstances may be uncongenial, but they shall not long remain so when you perceive an Ideal and strive to reach it.

Twenty-Third Morning

He who has conquered doubt and fear has con-quered failure. His every thought is allied with power, and all difficulties are bravely met and wisely overcome. His purposes are seasonably planted, and they bloom and bring forth fruit which does not fell prematurely to the ground.

Thought allied fearlessly to purpose becomes creative force: he who knows this is ready to become something higher and stronger than a mere bundle of wavering thoughts and fluctuating sensations; he who does this has become the con-scious and intelligent wielder of his mental powers.

Twenty-Third Evening

Man's true place in the Cosmos is that of a king, not a slave, a commander under the Law of Good, and not a helpless tool in the reign of evil.

I write for men, not for babes; for those who are eager to learn, and earnest to achieve; for those who will put away (for the world's good) a petty personal indulgence, a selfish desire, a mean thought, and live on as though it were not, sans craving and regret.

Man is a master. If he were not, he could not act contrary to law.

Evil and weakness are self destructive.

The universe is girt with goodness and strength, and it protects the good and the strong.

The angry man is the weak man.

Twenty-Fourth Morning

Not by learning will a man triumph over evil; not by much study will he overcome sin and sorrow. Only by conquering himself will he conquer evil; only by practising righteousness will he put an end to sorrow.

Not for the clever, nor the learned, nor the self-confident is the Life Triumphant, but for the pure, the virtuous and wise. The former achieve their particular success in life, but the latter alone achieve the great success so invincible and complete that even in apparent defeat it shines with added victory.

Twenty-Fourth Evening

The true silence is not merely a silent tongue; it is a silent mind. To merely hold one's tongue, and yet to carry about a disturbed and rankling mind, is no remedy for weakness, and no source of power. Silentness, to be powerful, must envelop the whole mind, must permeate every chamber of the heart; it must be the silence of peace. To this broad, deep, abiding silentness a man attains only in the measure that he conquers himself.

Twenty-Fifth Morning

By curbing his tongue, a man gains possession of his mind. The fool babbles, gossips, argues, and bandies words. He glories in the fact that he has had the last word, and has silenced his opponent. He exults in his own folly, is ever on the defensive, and wastes his energies in unprofitable channels. He is like a gardener who continues to dig and plant in unproductive soil.

The wise man avoids idle words, gossip, vain argument, and self-defence. He is content to appear defeated; rejoices when he is defeated; knowing that, having found and removed another error in himself he has thereby become wiser.

Blessed is he who does not strive for the last word.

Twenty-Fifth Evening

Desire is *the craving for possession*; aspiration is the *hunger of the heart for peace.* The craving things leads ever farther and farther from peace, and not only ends in deprivation, but is in itself a state of perpetual want. Until it comes to an end, rest and satisfaction are impossible. The hunger for things can never be satisfied, but the hunger for peace can, and the satisfaction of peace is found—is fully possessed, when all selfish desire is abandoned. Then there is fulness of joy, abounding plenty, and rich and complete blessedness.

Twenty-Sixth Morning

A man will reach the Kingdom by purifying himself, and he can only do this by pursuing a process of self-examination and self-analysis. The selfishness must be discovered and understood before it can be removed. It is powerless to remove itself, neither will it pass away of itself. Darkness ceases only when light is introduced; so ignorance can only be dispersed by knowledge, selfishness by love. A man must first of all be willing to lose himself (his self-seeking) before he can find himself (his Divine Self). He must realize that selfishness is not worth clinging to, that it is a master altogether unworthy of his service, and that divine goodness alone is worthy to be enthroned in his heart, as the supreme master of his life.

Twenty-Sixth Evening

Be still my soul, and know that peace is thine.
Be steadfast, heart, and know that strength divine
Belongs to thee; cease from thy turmoil, mind,
And thou the Everlasting Rest shalt find.

If a man would have peace, let him exercise the spirit of peace; if he would find Love, let him dwell in the spirit of Love; if he would escape suffering, let him cease to inflict it; if he would do noble things for humanity, let him cease to do ignoble things for himself. If he will but quarry the mine of his own soul, he shall find there all the materials for building whatsoever he will, and he shall find there also the Central Rock on which to build in safety.

Twenty-Seventh Morning

Men go after much company, and seek out new excitements, but they are not acquainted with peace; in divers paths of pleasure they search for happiness, but they do not come to rest; through diverse ways of laughter and feverish delirium they wander after gladness and life, but their tears are many and grievous, and they do not escape death.

Drifting upon the ocean of life in search of selfish indulgences, men are caught in its storms, and only after many tempests and much privation do they fly to the Rock of Refuge which rests in the deep silence of their own being.

Twenty-Seventh Evening

Meditation centered upon divine realities is the very essence and soul of prayer. It is the silent reaching upward of the soul toward the Eternal.

Meditation is the intense dwelling, in thought, upon an idea or theme with the object of thoroughly comprehending it; and whatsoever you constantly meditate upon, you will not only come to understand, but will grow more and more into its likeness, for it will become incorporated with your very being, will become, in fact, your very self. If, therefore, you constantly dwell upon that which is selfish and debasing, you will ultimately become selfish and debased; if you ceaselessly think upon that which is pure and unselfish, you will surely become pure and unselfish.

Twenty-Eighth Morning

There is no difficulty, however great, but will yield before a calm and powerful concentration of thought, and no legitimate object but may be speedily actualized by the intelligent use and direction of one's soul forces.

Whatever your task may be, concentrate your whole mind upon it; throw into it all the energy of which you are capable. The faultless completion of small tasks leads inevitably to larger tasks. See to it that you rise by steady climbing, and you will never fall.

Twenty-Eighth Evening

He who knows that Love is at the heart of all things, and has realized the all-sufficing power of that Love, has no room in his heart for condemnation.

If you love people, and speak of them with praise, until they in some way thwart you, or do something of which you disapprove, and then you dislike them and speak of them with dispraise, you are not governed by the Love which is of God. If, in your heart, you are continually arraigning and condemning others, selfless love is hidden from you.

Train your mind in strong, impartial, and gentle thought; train your heart in purity and compassion; train your tongue to silence, and to true and stainless speech; so shall you enter the way of holiness and peace, and shall ultimately realize the immortal Love.

Twenty-Ninth Morning

If you would realize true prosperity, do not settle down, as many have done, into the belief that if you do right everything will go wrong. Do not allow the word "competition" to shake your faith in the supremacy of righteousness. I care not what men may say about the "laws of competition," for do not I know the Unchangeable Law which shall one day put them all to rout, and which puts them to rout even now in the heart and life of the righteous man? And knowing this law I can contemplate all dishonesty with undisturbed repose, for I know where certain destruction awaits it.

Under all circumstances do *that which you believe to be right*, and trust the Law; trust the Divine Power which is immanent in the universe, and it will never desert you, and you will always be protected.

Twenty-Ninth Evening

Forget yourself entirely in the sorrows of others, in ministering to others, and divine happiness will emancipate you from all sorrow and suffering. "Taking the first step with a good thought, the second with a good word, and the third with a good deed, I entered Paradise." And you also enter Paradise by pursuing the same course.

Lose yourself in the welfare of others; forget yourself in all that you do—this is the secret of abounding happiness. Ever be on the watch to guard against selfishness, and learn faithfully the divine lessons of inward sacrifice; so shall you climb the highest heights of happiness, and shall remain in the never-clouded sunshine of universal joy, clothed in the shining garment of immortality.

Thirtieth Morning

When the farmer has tilled and dressed his land and put in the seed, he knows that he has done all that he can possibly do, and that now he must trust to the elements, and wait patiently for the course of time to bring about the harvest, and that no amount of expectancy on his part will affect the result. Even so, he who has realized Truth, goes forth as a sower of the seeds of goodness, purity, love, and peace, without expectancy, and never looking for results, knowing that there is the Great Over-ruling Law which brings about its own harvest in due time, and which is alike the source of preservation and destruction.

Thirtieth Evening

The virtuous put a check upon themselves, and set a watch upon their passions and emotions; in this way they gain possession of the mind, and gradually acquire calmness; and as they acquire influence, power, greatness, abiding joy, and fulness and completeness of life.

He only finds peace who conquers himself, who strives, day by day, after greater self-possession, greater self-control, greater calmness of mind.

Where the calm mind is, there is strength and rest, there is love and wisdom; there is one who has fought successfully innumerable battles against self, who, after long toil in secret against his own failings, has triumphed at last.

Thirty-First Morning

Sympathy bestowed increases its store in our own hearts, and enriches and fructifies our own life. Sympathy given is blessedness received; sympathy withheld is blessedness forfeited. In the measure that a man increases and enlarges his sympathy, so much nearer does he approach the ideal life, the perfect blessedness; and when his heart has become so mellowed that no hard, bitter, or cruel thought can enter and detract from its permanent sweetness, then indeed is he richly and divinely blessed.

Thirty-First Evening

Sweet is the rest and deep the bliss of him who has freed his heart from its lusts and hatreds and dark desires; and he who, without any shadow of bitterness resting upon him, and looking out upon the world with boundless compassion and love, can breathe, in his inmost heart, the blessing:

Peace unto all living things,

making no exceptions or distinctions—such a man has reached that happy ending which can never be taken away, for this is the perfection of life, the fulness of peace, the consummation of perfect blessedness.

James Allen: A Memoir

By Lily L. Allen

from *The Epoch* (February–March 1912)

> *Unto pure devotion*
> *Devote thyself: with perfect meditation*
> *Comes perfect act, and the right-hearted rise—*
> *More certainly because they seek no gain—*
> *Forth from the bands of body, step by step.*
> *To highest seats of bliss.*

James Allen was born in Leicester, England, on November 28th, 1864. His father, at one time a very prosperous manufacturer, was especially fond of "Jim," and before great financial failures overtook him, he would often look at the delicate, refined boy, poring over his books, and would say, "My boy, I'll make a scholar of you."

The Father was a high type of man intellectually, and a great reader, so could appreciate the evident thirst for education and knowledge which he observed in his quiet studious boy.

As a young child he was very delicate and nervous, often suffering untold agony during his school days through the misunderstanding harshness of some of his school teachers, and others with whom he was forced to associate, though he retained always the tenderest memories of others—one or two of his teachers in particular, who no doubt are still living.

He loved to get alone with his books, and many a time he has drawn a vivid picture for me, of the hours he spent with his precious books in his favourite corner by the home fire; his father, whom he dearly loved, in his arm chair opposite also deeply engrossed in his favourite authors. On such evenings he would question his father on some of the profound thoughts that surged through his soul— thoughts he could scarcely form into words—and the father, unable to answer, would gaze at him long over his spectacles, and at last say: "My boy, my boy, you have lived before"—and when the boy eagerly but reverently would suggest an answer to his own question, the father would grow silent and thoughtful, as though he *sensed* the future man and his mission, as he looked at the boy and listened to his words—and many a time he was heard to remark, "Such knowledge comes not in one short life."

There were times when the boy startled those about him into a deep concern for his health, and they would beg him not to *think so much*, and in after years he often smiled when he recalled how his father would say—"Jim, we will have you in the Churchyard soon, if you think so much."

Not that he was by any means unlike other boys where games were concerned. He could play leap-frog and marbles with the best of them, and those who knew him as a man—those who were privileged to meet him at "Bryngoleu"—will remember how he could enter into a game with all his heart. Badminton he delighted in during the summer evenings, or whenever he felt he could.

About three years after our marriage, when our little Nora was about eighteen months old, and he about thirty-three, I realized a great change coming over him, and knew that he was renouncing everything that most men hold dear that he might find Truth, and lead the weary sin-stricken world to Peace. He at that time commenced the practice of rising early in the morning, at times long before daylight, that he might go out on the hills—like One of old—to commune with God, and meditate on Divine things. I do not claim to have understood him fully in those days. The light in which he lived and moved was far too white for my earth-bound eyes to see, and a *sense of it only* was beginning to dawn upon me. But I knew I dare not stay him or hold him back, though at times my woman's heart cried out to do so, waiting him all my own, and not then understanding his divine mission.

Then came his first book, "From Poverty to Power." This book is considered by many his best book. It has passed into many editions, and tens of thousands have been sold all over the world, both authorized and pirated editions, for perhaps no author's works have been more pirated than those of James Allen.

As a private secretary he worked from 9 a.m. to 6 p.m., and used every moment out of office writing his books. Soon after the publication of "From Poverty to Power" came "All These Things Added," and then "As a Man Thinketh," a book perhaps better known and more widely read than any other from his pen.

About this time, too, the "Light of Reason" was founded and he gave up all his time to the work of editing the Magazine, at the same time carrying on a voluminous correspondence with searchers after Truth all over the world. And ever as the years went by he kept straight on, and never once looked back or swerved from the path of holiness. Oh, it was a blessed thing indeed to be the chosen one to walk by the side of his earthly body, and to watch the glory dawning upon him!

He took a keen interest in many scientific subjects, and always eagerly read the latest discovery in astronomy, and he delighted in geology and botany. Among his favourite books I find Shakespeare, Milton, Emerson, Browning, The Bhagavad-Gita, the Tao-Tea-King of Lao-Tze, the Light of Asia, the Gospel of Buddha, Walt Whitman, Dr. Bucke's Cosmic Consciousness, and the Holy Bible.

He might have written on a wide range of subjects had he chosen to do so, and was often asked for articles on many questions outside his particular work, but he refused to comply, consecrating his whole thought and effort to preach the Gospel of Peace.

When physical suffering overtook him he never once complained, but grandly and patiently bore his pain, hiding it from those around him, and only we who knew and loved him so well, and his kind, tender Doctor, knew how greatly he suffered. And yet he stayed not; still he rose before the dawn to meditate, and commune with God; still he sat at his desk and wrote those words of Light and Life which will ring down through the ages, calling men and women from their sins and sorrows to peace and rest.

Always strong in his complete manhood, though small of stature physically, and as gentle as he was strong, no one ever heard an angry word from those kind lips. Those who served him adored him; those who had business dealings with him trusted and honoured him. Ah! how much my heart prompts me to write of his self-sacrificing life, his tender words, his gentle deeds, his knowledge and his wisdom. But why? Surely there is no need, for do not his books speak in words written by his own hand, and will they not speak to generations yet to come?

About Christmas time I saw the change coming, and understood it not—blind! blind! blind! I could not think it possible that *he* should be taken and *I* left.

But we three—as if we knew—clung closer to each other, and loved one another with a greater love—if that were possible—than ever before. Look at his portrait given with the January "Epoch," and reproduced again in this, and you will see that even then our Beloved, our Teacher and Guide, was letting go his hold on the physical. He was leaving us then, and we didn't know it. Often I had urged him to stop work awhile and rest, but he always gave me the same answer, "My darling, when I stop I must go, don't try to stay my hand."

And so he worked on, until that day, Friday, January 12, 1912, when, about one o'clock he sat down in his chair, and looking at me with a great compassion and yearning in those blessed eyes, he cried out, as he stretched out his arms to me, *"Oh, I have finished, I have finished, I can go no further, I have done."*

Need I say that everything that human aid and human skill could do was done to keep him still with us. Of those last few days I dare scarcely write. How could my pen describe them? And when we knew the end was near, with his dear hands upon my head in blessing, he gave his work and his beloved people into my hands, charging me to bless and help them, until I received the call to give up my stewardship!

"I will help you," he said, "and if I can I shall come to you and be with you often."

Words, blessed words of love and comfort, *for my heart alone* often came from his lips, and a sweet smile ever came over the pale calm face when our little Nora came to kiss him and speak loving words to him, while always the gentle voice breathed the tender words to her—*"My little darling!"*

So calmly, peacefully, quietly, he passed from us at the dawn on Wednesday, January 24, 1912. "Passed from us," did I say? Nay, only the outer garment has passed from our mortal vision. He lives! and when the great grief that tears our hearts at the separation is calmed and stilled, I think that we shall know that he is still with us. We shall again rejoice in his companionship and presence.

When his voice was growing faint and low, I heard him whispering, and leaning down to catch the words I heard—"At last, at last—at home— my wanderings are over"—and then, I heard no more, for my heart was breaking within me, and I felt, for *him* indeed it was *"Home at last!"* but for me—And then, as though he knew my thoughts, he turned and again holding out his hands to me, he said: "I have only one thing more to say to you, my beloved, and that is I love you, and I will be waiting for you; good-bye."

I write this memoir for those who love him, for those who will read it with tender loving hearts, and tearful eyes; for those who will not look critically at the way in which I have tried to tell out of my lonely heart this short story of his life and passing away—for *his* pupils, and, therefore, my friends.

We clothed the mortal remains in *pure white linen*, symbol of his fair, pure life, and so, clasping the photo of the one he loved best upon his bosom—they committed all that remained to the funeral pyre.

About the Author

James Allen was one of the pioneering figures of the self-help movement and modern inspirational thought. A philosophical writer and poet, he is best known for his book *As a Man Thinketh*. Writing about complex subjects such as faith, destiny, love, patience, and religion, he had the unique ability to explain them in a way that is simple and easy to comprehend. He often wrote about cause and effect, as well as overcoming sadness, sorrow and grief.

Allen was born in 1864 in Leicester, England into a working-class family. His father travelled alone to America to find work, but was murdered within days of arriving. With the family now facing economic disaster, Allen, at age 15, was forced to leave school and find work to support them.

During stints as a private secretary and stationer, he found that he could showcase his spiritual and social interests in journalism by writing for the magazine *The Herald of the Golden Age.*

In 1901, when he was 37, Allen published his first book, *From Poverty to Power.* In 1902 he began to publish his own spiritual magazine, *The Light of Reason* (which would be retitled *The Epoch* after his death). Each issue contained announcements, an editorial written by Allen on a different subject each month, and many articles, poems, and quotes written by popular authors of the day and even local, unheard of authors.

His third and most famous book *As a Man Thinketh* was published in 1903. The book's minor popularity enabled him to quit his secretarial work and pursue his writing and editing career full time. He wrote 19 books in all, publishing at least one per year while continuing to publish his magazine, until his death. Allen wrote when he had a message—one that he had lived out in his own life and knew that it was good.

In 1905, Allen organized his magazine subscribers into groups (called "The Brotherhood") that would meet regularly and reported on their meetings each month in the magazine. Allen and his wife, Lily Louisa Oram, whom he had married in 1895, would often travel to these group meetings to give speeches and read articles. Some of Allen's favorite writings, and those he quoted often, include the works of Shakespeare, Milton, Emerson, the Bible, Buddha, Whitman, Trine, and Lao-Tze.

Allen died in 1912 at the age of 47. Following his death, Lily, with the help of their daughter, Nora took over the editing of *The Light of Reason*, now under the name *The Epoch*. Lily continued to publish the magazine until her failing eyesight prevented her from doing so. Lily's life was devoted to spreading the works of her husband until her death at age 84.

Printed in the USA
CPSIA information can be obtained
at www.ICGtesting.com
JSHW012045140824
68134JS00034B/3270